The Restless Sea

UNDERWATER EXPLORATION

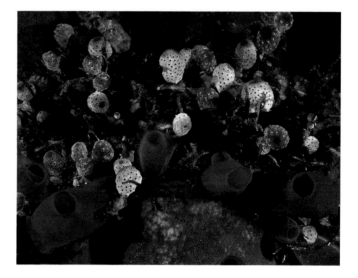

CAROLE GARBUNY VOGEL

Franklin Watts®

A Division of Scholastic Inc.
New York • Toronto • London • Auckland • Sydney
Mexico City • New Delhi • Hong Kong
Danbury, Connecticut

FOR JESSICA HELD

ACKNOWLEDGMENTS

Many thanks to Professor Peter Guth, Oceanography Department, U.S. Naval Academy, who took time from his busy schedule to read and critique the manuscript, and answer my many questions. His vast knowledge of the field and keen insight were reflected in his comments.

I am indebted to Milton Butterworth, photographer/videographer for the Columbus-America Discovery Group, for supplying photographs and for reviewing the text concerning the shipwreck of the SS *Central America* and the discovery of its ruins.

I am also grateful to fellow writer Dr. Joyce A. Nettleton for her invaluable criticism, scientific expertise, and sense of humor. Special thanks to students Stephen, Daniel, and Joanna Guth for reading the manuscript from the kid perspective. I especially appreciate the report that Stephen prepared, detailing what worked and what didn't.

My sincere appreciation to my husband, Mark A. Vogel, for the encouragement and understanding that has become his hallmark. I would also like to acknowledge the help of the many other people who helped either directly or indirectly.

Finally, my heartfelt thanks to my editor, Kate Nunn, for having faith in my writing ability and the talent to turn my manuscripts into spectacular books.

Book design by Marie O'Neill

Library of Congress Cataloging-in-Publication Data

Vogel, Carole Garbuny.
  Underwater exploration / Carole G. Vogel.
    p. cm. — (The restless sea)
Summary: Explores the treasures found in the deep sea and introduces
scientists who have learned to map the oceans with manned submersibles
and underwater robots.
Includes bibliographical references and index.
  ISBN 0-531-12327-8 (lib. bdg.)   0-531-16684-8 (pbk.)
  1. Underwater exploration—Juvenile literature. [1. Underwater
exploration.] I. Title.
  GC65.V64 2003
  551.46'07—dc21
        2003005306

contents

chapter 1

UNDERWATER TREASURE HUNT

On August 20, 1857, at the height of the California gold rush, about 475 passengers bound for New York boarded the steamship SS *Sonora* in San Francisco. An estimated 21 tons (19,000 kilograms) of gold in the form of gold dust, bars, coins, and nuggets were brought aboard. The gold was worth tens of millions of dollars at the time, which is equivalent to hundreds of millions now. According to military documents from that era, 15 tons (13,600 kilograms) of the gold were contained in a secret U.S. Army shipment intended to bolster the sagging economy in the North. The rest belonged to the travelers or New York banks.

The first leg of the journey lasted two weeks and took the vessel south from San Francisco to the Isthmus of Panama. This narrow strip of land is part of a thin sliver connecting North and South Americas. Mostly jungle, it separates the Atlantic and Pacific Oceans. In Panama the passengers and precious cargo were transferred from a port on the Pacific side to a train that crossed Panama in three and a half hours. Awaiting them on the Atlantic coast was the SS *Central America* and its 101-member crew.

The *Central America* was a side-wheel steamer—a long coal-powered ship with a paddle wheel three stories high on each side. To enhance speed and handling, the vessel was equipped with three masts and sails. Its anticipated travel time between Panama and New York was nine days. Although this complicated journey from California to New York took almost a month, it was far quicker than the other options available—crossing North America by wagon or sailing around the tip of South America.

On September 3, the *Central America* cast off from Panama with the cargo and most of the transferred passengers. A few travelers may have chosen to stay behind in Panama. The first four days aboard the *Central America* passed uneventfully as the ship cruised through calm seas and sweltering hot tropical air.

A painting of the SS *Central America*

On September 7, it made a scheduled overnight layover in Havana, Cuba, to pick up coal and provisions. The next day, after the ship had been under way for several hours, a stiff breeze began to ruffle the water. Gentle swells gradually gave way to angry, hulking waves.

A blood-red sunset heralded the approach of turbulent weather. By the next afternoon, rain pelted down in sheets. The waves were the size of small hills. Howling winds churned the water into a froth, painting the air white with foam. With each wave the boat rocked up and down, seesawlike. Nauseous, most passengers either retched over the railing or retired to their berths. Some vomited in the cramped quarters below deck, fouling the air and contributing to the seasickness of others. Accustomed to bad weather at sea, the sailors carried out their tasks unperturbed. As long as the crew could keep the bow (the front part) of the ship headed into the wind, they believed they could ride out any storm.

By the third day out of Havana, the wind was blowing at hurricane force. The waves towered over the ship and even the seasoned sailors became jittery. They realized they were confronting a monster storm.

Dawn of the fourth day brought no relief. The force of the wind intensified, and the vessel began to take on water, tilting to one side. That afternoon the water rose so high in the hold that it extinguished the fire in both boilers. The paddle wheels stopped turning, and the ship could no longer be steered. Now at the whim of the waves, the listing ship was in danger of sinking.

William Herndon, the ship's captain, ordered all the male passengers to form a bucket brigade to bail out the ship. Some women wanted to help, but the men rebuffed them on the grounds that bailing was not women's work. Using wash buckets and water pitchers, the men bailed throughout the remainder of the day and through the night. Despite their valiant effort, they could not stay ahead of the water. Inch by inch it climbed higher.

Early the next morning, the wind died down and the sun broke through the clouds. Believing the worst was behind them, the exhausted men and beleaguered women rejoiced. But the respite was temporary. The ship was in the eye of the hurricane, a region of calm inside the raging storm. The brutal winds soon returned, more savage than ever. With each giant cresting wave, an avalanche of

This satellite image shows Hurricane Floyd, which devastated North Carolina in 1999. Floyd, one of the most destructive storms to strike the United States in modern times, was as powerful as the one that doomed the *Central America*.

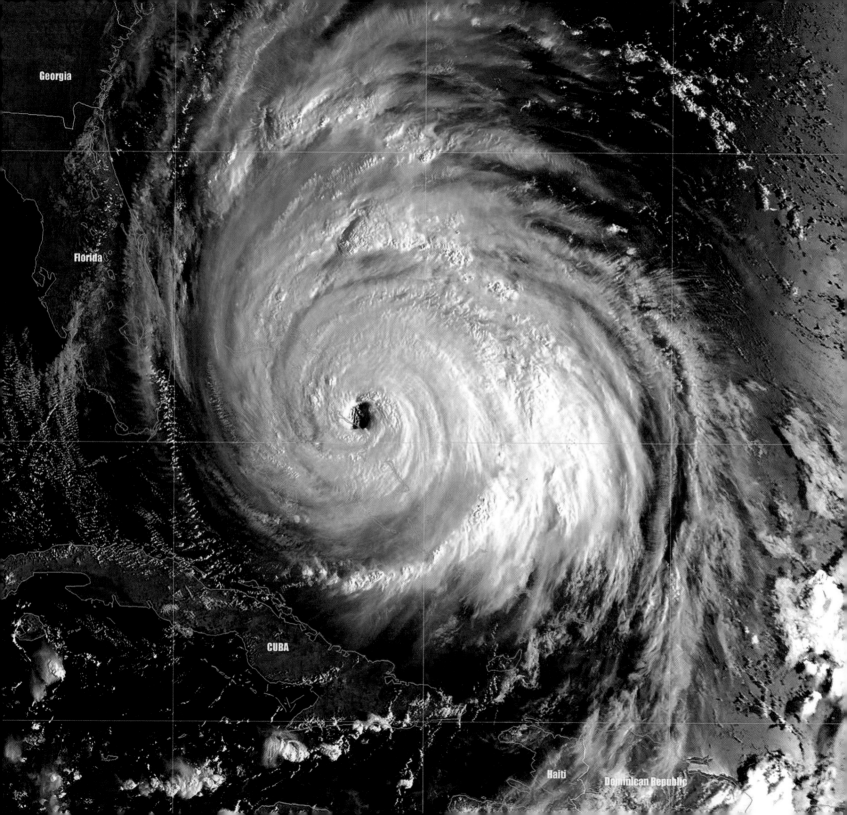

water crashed down on the ship. By noon, all hope of saving it was gone but the men kept bailing to buy time.

Around 2:00 P.M., the sinking ship was spotted by the *Marine*, a two-masted cargo ship less than half the size of the *Central America*. The hurricane had partially crippled the *Marine*. In the storm-tossed sea, its captain could not maintain a position close to the stricken vessel. The ships began to drift apart. Nevertheless all the women and children (except for one boy, who probably chose to remain with his 21-year-old brother) were transferred from the *Central America* to the *Marine* in three lifeboats. Slowed by mountainous waves, the round-trip between ships took several hours. By the time the lifeboats completed their second trip, the *Marine* had drifted so far away that there was no opportunity to rescue the remaining 478 male passengers and crew aboard the doomed ship. Life preservers were offered to the unfortunate ones left behind.

Panic and confusion reigned among the marooned men. Some prayed, others cursed, while still others screamed in terror. Many men set aside their love of gold, casting off their money belts stuffed with the precious but heavy metal. They knew they could not stay afloat with their treasure weighing them down.

After nightfall, the *Central America* slipped beneath the waves. The tremendous suction created by the sinking ship dragged the men down. Those who could break free returned to pandemonium at the surface. The water was littered with castaways—some living, some dead. In life preservers, they wobbled back and forth with the waves, like bobbers on fishing lines. The dead floated silently with their faces in the sea. The living kept their heads above water, some by clinging to debris. The roar of the angry ocean drowned out their cries of despair.

About five hours after the sinking, a Norwegian vessel chanced upon the shipwrecked men. The crew plucked 50 survivors from the water but were too late to save the rest. Another 3 men were found nine days later adrift in a lifeboat. All together, 153 people survived and an estimated 425 perished. In the aftermath the staggering loss of life and the immense value of the sunken gold captured the imagination of the American people. Survivors were besieged by newspaper reporters eager to publish eyewitness accounts.

The loss of so much gold contributed to one of the worst financial crises in the

United States, the Panic of 1857. New York banks, dependent on their share of the gold to back up loans, could not pay off their debts. The banks began to fail, causing a ripple effect. Stores and factories that had deposited money in the failed banks could not get their money back. Consequently, they could not meet their own payrolls. Soon they were forced to close, too, leaving their workers jobless.

RECOVERY IN THE DEEP

At first, salvaging the *Central America* and its gold treasure was impossible. The ship had settled in deep water 200 miles (322 kilometers) off the South Carolina coast. The technology for deep-sea recovery did not exist in the 1800s. More than a century would pass before experts in marine engineering tackled the problem of finding shipwrecks and recovering their artifacts. One of these ocean engineers was Tommy Thompson, who was born in Huntington, Indiana, in 1952. Since childhood Thompson has had an immense curiosity about how mechanical things worked and a talent for inventing devices. In college he focused on the mechanics of working in the deep ocean. By 1983, Thompson had decided that he wanted to find a shipwreck in deep water, explore and document it, and then recover the artifacts. Intrigued by the lost treasure and historical value of the *Central America*, he set his sights on this ill-fated ship. In 1985, Thompson formed a coalition called the Columbus-America Discovery Group to help realize his goal. This enterprise eventually included approximately 40 engineers, adventurers, and crew members, as well as 161 financial backers, who raised over $10 million for the project.

Thompson and his team used both historical data and modern-day technology to search for the wreck. They researched hundreds of accounts given by survivors and other eyewitnesses and scrutinized these reports for clues of the ship's path. The data was fed into computers, along with information on the effects of winds and currents. Using special computer-modeling techniques, the researchers identified probable routes of the *Central America*. They narrowed down the likely site of the wreck to a 1,400-square-mile (3,600-square-kilometer) region 200 miles (300 kilometers) from the South Carolina mainland, in water 1.5 miles (2.4 kilometers) deep.

The target area was more than 20 times larger than the city of Washington, D.C. To make the search more manageable, the area was divided up like a checkerboard with cells a half a mile square (1.3 kilometers square). Each cell was assigned a number based on the chance of the wreck being there. In the summer of 1986, Thompson and his team chartered a boat and equipped it with a side-scan sonar device to search the area, paying particular attention to the most probable cells.

Side-scan sonar produces pulses of sound waves that travel through the water to the sea bottom in a fan-shaped beam. This use of sound waves is some-what similar to focusing a flashlight beam on an object. But instead of light bouncing back and reaching the eyes, sound waves bounce back when they hit the bottom and return to the device. The device constructs an image by measuring the time it takes for the reflected sound waves to travel back. The farther away an object, the longer it takes for the echo to return.

Side-scan sonar can also provide detailed information about the make up of the seafloor and objects on it. When sound waves strike an object, they can be absorbed or scattered in different directions. For example, soft mud absorbs much more sound energy than hard rocks or wooden ship beams do. By measuring the intensity (amount of energy) in returning sound waves, a side-scan sonar device can discern texture. This information can be used to color the image.

For 40 days, the scientist-explorers conducted their survey. Towing the sonar device behind the ship in

10

straight lines, they crisscrossed the area, lawn-mower fashion. With each pass, the instrument scanned a 30-mile-long (48-kilometer), 3-mile-wide (4.9-kilometer) ribbon of seafloor. The team glimpsed several promising sites, but lacked the time to investigate them further. Their time at sea was limited by the weather window—the best months for good weather and calm seas—which lasts from early June to late October. Nevertheless they identified several promising sites.

The scientists devoted the following winter to analyzing the sonar images and building *Nemo*. *Nemo* was an undersea robot, technically known as a ROV—remotely operated vehicle. About the size of a pickup truck, *Nemo* looked like a cross between an Erector set and a junkyard sculpture. However, appearances can be deceiving. The ROV was more like a gigantic Swiss Army knife with a tool for every imaginable need. It was outfitted with powerful lights, cameras, and two mechanical arms. The "hands" of the arms could be changed depending on the task. Usually only the main arm was used. When equipped with a clawed manipulator at the end, the arm could lift large beams and heavy passenger trunks. For delicate operations, such as gathering individual gold coins, a suction device was attached to the arm. A robotic "hand" with padded fingers was used to pick up large gold bars without scratching them. A gentle vacuum attachment sucked up gold dust and other materials too tiny to be retrieved by other means. There was even a gadget that covered stacks of coins with silicone gel so they could be recovered intact. (The silicone gel hardened quickly and was peeled off after the coins were brought to the surface.) *Nemo* contained drawers and other storage compartments to hold the artifacts. All this equipment needed to be strong enough to withstand the crushing pressure of the deep ocean. To keep costs down, the ROV was built with as many off-the-shelf, inexpensive components as feasible.

In the summer of 1987, *Nemo* got its first test before it was completely rigged. Tethered to a ship at the surface by 14,000 feet (4,270 meters) of coaxial cable, the ROV was lowered to the seafloor. The cable allowed the ROV to transmit information from its cameras and sensors to computers on the mother ship. And it permitted scientists monitoring the computers to give instructions to *Nemo*. The ROV recovered a lump of coal from a sunken ship. Unfortunately the ship wasn't the *Central America*. The team had already lost time that summer

A winch on the mother ship carefully lowered *Nemo* 8,000 feet (2,440 m) to the ocean bottom, a process that took 90 minutes. The ship not only served as a launching pad and repair shop for *Nemo*, but also provided work space, dining facilities, and a dormitory for Tommy Thompson and his team.

13

exploring another shipwreck, which proved to be too small to be the *Central America*. Now it was too late in the season to explore additional sites.

That winter, further scrutiny of the sonar images revealed a third promising site. Although eager to explore it, Thompson and his team experienced a frustrating delay the next summer while they waited for critical parts for their new mother ship. *Nemo* made its first dive of the season on September 11, 1988. The ROV's cameras revealed an enormous rusting paddle wheel lying in the mud. The next day the ship's bell was discovered, confirming the identity of the *Central America*. Technical glitches and rough seas slowed exploration of the wreck. So a couple weeks passed before the lost treasure was located. Amid rotting timbers and coal lay heaps and heaps of gold coins and bars. Around the wreck, gold was scattered helter-skelter, carpeting the seafloor like a garden gone to seed. Some of the coins were sparkling and had no scratches, as if they had been minted the day before. Among them were rare 1857 double eagles—twenty-dollar gold pieces—and even rarer fifty-dollar gold pieces minted in 1851. These coins are especially prized by coin collectors. The serious recovery work began in 1989, and most of the gold has since been brought to the surface.

The chilly water (a few degrees above freezing) had turned the shipwreck into a giant refrigerator, preserving the possessions of the crew and passengers, as well as other items on the ship. Some of these artifacts have been retrieved, providing a glimpse into the past. Among them was a large leather trunk that had belonged to newlyweds Ansel and Adeline Easton, both of whom survived the shipwreck. The trunk held linen shirts, vests, trousers, petticoats, bloomers, robes, and stockings, as well as many other articles of clothing. It also contained a pair of dueling pistols, a gunpowder flask, a Chinese carving, three bottles of cologne, two quill pens, and a quartz watch.

So why did it take more than 130 years to recover the gold and other artifacts aboard the *Central America*?

A small sampling of the treasure found among the ruins of the *Central America*

Inset: *Nemo* placed collection trays on the seafloor in preparation for retrieving the lost gold. When filled, the collection trays were placed in a drawer inside *Nemo* for the return trip to the mother ship.

14

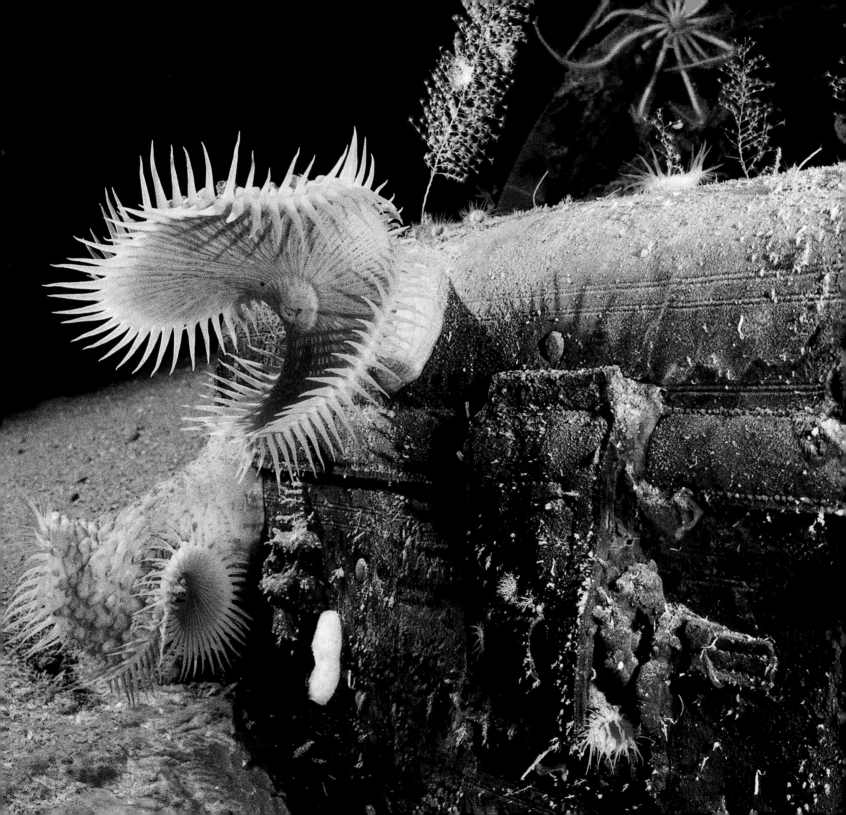

CENTRAL AMERICA FINDS

The wreck of the *Central America* served as a time capsule for the tools, clothing, toiletries, weapons, and other products commonly used during the 1850s.

Clockwise from the top: a gold and quartz fob (a holder for a pocket watch), a man's fancy linen dress shirt, a man's waistcoat (vest) with a silk front, a pair of Derringer pistols, a leather trunk (now covered by orange sea anemones and plumy golden coral)

chapter 2

THE HIDDEN FRONTIER

More people have traveled to the moon than have ventured to the bottom of the ocean's deepest spot, the Mariana Trench. The Mariana Trench is a spectacular gash in the seafloor nearly 7 miles (11 kilometers) below the surface of the Pacific Ocean, southwest of Guam. At the trench's lowest point, the pressure of the overlying water on a human body is equivalent to the weight of a stack of 50 jumbo jets. So far, only two people have braved the journey into the abyss. In 1960, U.S. Navy Lieutenant Donald Walsh and Swiss researcher Jacques Piccard descended into the depths aboard the bathyscaphe *Trieste*.

The bathyscaphe consisted of a cramped passenger compartment (a hollow steel ball) attached to a large flotation device (a gasoline-filled container resembling a submarine). Sixteen tons of iron pellets provided the weight needed to pull the bathyscaphe into the deep. The voyage down lasted five hours, and the *Trieste* remained on the bottom for only 20 minutes. This was long enough for the explorers to glimpse an ivory-colored flatfish through a tiny porthole.

The *Trieste* couldn't crawl along the seafloor or retrieve objects. Like an elevator, it was only capable of up-and-down movement. To return to the surface, the crew released the iron pellets. The gasoline in the flotation device was lighter than seawater and enabled the vessel to rise to the surface. In 1963 the navy retired the *Trieste*. So far, no other manned vehicle can dive as deep. But in 1995, Japanese scientists successfully sent *Kaiko*, a $60 million ROV, to probe the Mariana Trench.

UNDISCOVERED COUNTRY
The ocean basin is not large enough to contain all of the ocean's water. The overflow covers the continental shelf, the apron of gently sloping land that fringes the continents. The water brimming over the shelf is relatively shallow and rarely

The bathyscaphe *Trieste* was built in 1953 by the father-and-son team of Auguste and Jacques Piccard. The U.S. Navy purchased it five years later.

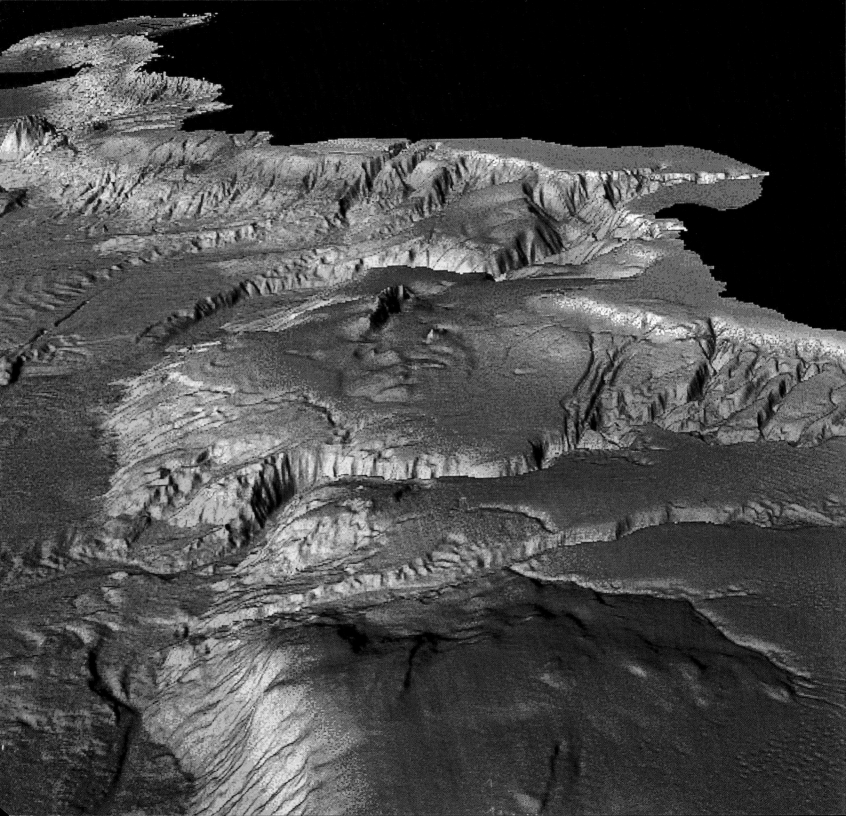

reaches a depth greater than 650 feet (200 meters). The continental shelf terminates abruptly in a steep cliff called the continental slope. The slope drops down about 13,000 feet (4,000 meters) to the abyssal plain on the deep-sea floor. The abyssal plain is flat, vast, and covered by sediments—mud, clay, and debris from living things. Oozes—the mushy remains of plants and animals—shroud about half of the deep-sea floor. The sediments are thickest close to the continents, where they accumulate rapidly. Far from land the accumulation rate is extremely slow and sediment thickness varies with the age of the seafloor. The younger the seafloor, the thinner its sediment blanket.

The featureless landscape of the abyssal plain is interrupted by steep-sided gorges deeper than the Grand Canyon and majestic mountains more imposing than the Rockies. Along one stretch of the Pacific seafloor more than 1,100 volcanoes and seamounts pepper an area the size of New York State. Tucked far beneath the ocean's surface, all this magnificent terrain remains largely unexplored because of the expense and peril. Although the ocean covers nearly 71 percent of Earth's surface, scientists know more about the celestial realm— the Sun, Moon, and stars—than they know about the depths of the sea. The extreme pressure, absence of breathable air, and cold temperatures render deep-sea exploration as dangerous as space travel.

THE BIG CRUSH

We live at the bottom of a colossal ocean of air—the atmosphere. Billions of air molecules constantly push on you from every direction. At sea level the atmosphere presses on you with a force of nearly 15 pounds per square inch (1 kilogram per square centimeter). It doesn't squash you because your body is adapted to withstand it. The human body, however, is not designed to tolerate the pressure of water in the deep. If you have ever carried a large jug of water, you know that water is heavy. Since water is much heavier than air, it presses down with more force. The pressure increases with depth.

If a scuba diver descends just 33 feet (10 meters) in the ocean, the sheer weight of the water alone exerts a pressure equal to that of the atmosphere. The diver then experiences the combined pressure of the atmosphere and water. If the diver

This sonar map shows the continental shelf and deep-sea floor off the California coast. Colors show depth. White areas are near sea level, orange areas are 3,200 feet (1,000 m) deep, yellow are 6,400 feet (2,000 m) deep, and blue regions have a depth of 9,600 feet (3,000 m).

descends another 33 feet (10 meters), the water pressure by itself equals that of two atmospheres. The pressure increases in this fashion all the way to the seafloor. Divers are cautioned not to descend below 130 feet (40 meters) because of the risk of serious injury.

Two miles (3.2 kilometers) down, the pressure exceeds 4,000 pounds per square inch (290 kilograms per square centimeter), a force great enough to crush a human instantly. Nevertheless a multitude of organisms thrive in this high-pressure realm. They are as well adapted to their environment as you are to yours. If these creatures were taken to the surface, their bodies would explode. If the atmosphere suddenly disappeared, your body would swell although it would not explode. With no oxygen to breathe, however, death would come quickly.

Scuba gear—a tank containing compressed air and a regulator to supply the air at a safe pressure—was invented in 1939. It solved the problem of beathing underwater and allows divers to swim freely to depths greater than 100 feet (30 m). Scuba stands for self-contained underwater breathing apparatus. The scuba diver here is shown with a green moray eel.

Aches and Pains of Air Pressure

Atmospheric pressure is greatest at sea level since the air there has the weight of the entire atmosphere pressing down on it. The pressure decreases with altitude. The summit of Alaska's Mount Saint Elias (the second highest mountain in the United States) soars 18,000 feet (5,490 meters) above sea level. There, the air pressure is about 7.3 pounds per square inch (.5 kilogram per square centimeter) or half the air pressure at the shore. About 50 percent of the atmosphere's molecules are above this elevation and the remainder are below. At this altitude you could easily become winded because with each breath you would take in half as many oxygen molecules as you do at sea level.

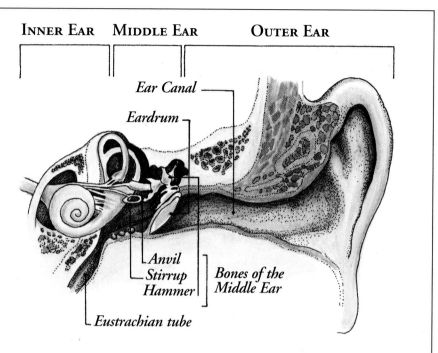

INNER EAR   MIDDLE EAR   OUTER EAR

Ear Canal

Eardrum

Anvil
Stirrup
Hammer

Bones of the
Middle Ear

Eustachian tube

You are usually oblivious of the force of the atmosphere pressing down on you. However, your ears can make you aware of rapid changes in air pressure. Your outer ear consists of the visible part plus the ear canal, a tube that leads to your eardrum. The eardrum is a thin tissue that stretches across the end of the ear canal. Behind the eardrum lie air spaces and the bones of the middle ear. The eustachian tube, a passageway about the width of a pencil lead, connects the air spaces in the middle ear to the back of the nose. The eustachian tube controls the flow of air to the middle ear. Usually it keeps the air pressure on both sides of the eardrum in balance.

Sometimes when you ride in an elevator or airplane, your ears can't adjust quickly enough to air-pressure changes. The eustachian tubes become clogged. If you are rising in elevation, the pressure in the middle ear is higher than the outside pressure. So the eardrum bulges outward. If you are descending, the air pressure in the middle ear is lower. The eardrum bends inward. In either case, your ears may feel blocked or you might experience a sharp pain. Swallowing or yawning can help your ears pop, equalizing the pressure.

PICTURING THE OCEAN WITH SOUND

It is ironic that you can see the Sun, which is approximately 93 million miles (150 million kilometers) away, yet you cannot see far in seawater. Light from the Sun passes through the boundless vacuum of outer space but when it strikes the ocean, tiny suspended particles in seawater reflect and absorb it. More than half of the visible light penetrating the sea is absorbed within 3 feet (.9 meter) of the surface. By a depth of 33 feet (10 meters), about 80 percent of the light has vanished. Even in the clearest waters, only 1 percent of the light extends below 500 feet (150 meters). At depths of 3,300 feet (1,000 meters) or greater, water is coal-black. Consequently three-fourths of the ocean is cloaked in unending darkness.

Sound waves carry well in water. So fish and other marine creatures picture their surroundings using sound waves instead of light. Sound waves are vibrations that are created when an object moves. The vibrations zip away from the source, just as waves ripple outward when you plunk a pebble into a pond.

Sound waves travel though the bodies of fish to their inner ears. There, the vibrations are translated into nerve impulses and transmitted to the auditory hearing center of the brain, where they are interpreted. Fish rely on hearing for detecting faraway sounds in their surroundings. For detecting nearby sounds, they depend on their lateral-line sense, a mix of hearing and touch. A lateral line consists of a series of fluid-filled tubes running in a row from head to tail beneath the skin on each side of a fish. The lateral-line sense organs interpret vibrations as waves of pressure and enable fish to sense the direction of water flow, detect predators, find prey, and maintain position in a school. Humans have no counterpart for this sense.

Dolphins use sound waves in an even more sophisticated way, called echolocation, to position themselves and detect objects. Echolocation is a natural form of sonar. Dolphins produce sound waves—usually high-frequency clicks—that speed through the water, bounce off objects, and return as echoes. The time it takes for the echo to return depends on the distance. The dolphin processes the information to make a picture of its surroundings.

The lateral lines of cottonmouth jacks are highly visible near the base of their tails.

MAPPING THE SEAFLOOR

In the 1920s, the invention of the first successful sonar devices for measuring the depths of the seafloor made possible the mapping of the ocean bottom. These devices were quite primitive, producing hazy images. A comprehensive worldwide survey of the ocean floor didn't begin until the 1950s. Then, improved imaging technology developed during World War II for hunting enemy submarines became available.

Detailed examination of the seafloor revealed the existence of numerous steep-walled trenches—canyons—in the Pacific Ocean (and significantly fewer trenches in the other oceans). The seafloor surveys also showed a ribbon of rugged mountains running through every ocean basin. This globe-circling mountain range is known as the mid-ocean ridge. It is submerged under thousands of feet of water for most of its 40,000-mile (65,000-kilometer) length. The highest peaks soar through the ocean's ceiling, creating islands such as Iceland in the Atlantic and Easter Island in the Pacific.

If the mid-ocean ridge were not concealed by water, it would be the most conspicuous landform on the planet. The ridge covers nearly as much territory as the dry land of all the continents combined. In places where the underwater ranges loom steep and narrow, a V-shaped valley extends the length of the ridge. Known as rift valleys, these drowned gorges are the longest valleys in the world. They are slit down the center by a deep rift (crack) that bubbles with volcanic activity. In some parts of the mountain chain, wider and gentler mountains, called rises, appear. Rises lack rift valleys but a lava-oozing rift wends across their summits. More than 80 percent of Earth's volcanic eruptions take place along the mid-ocean ridge. All together, the submerged volcanoes pour out enough lava each year to cover Canada and the continental United States in a coating 1 foot (30 centimeters) thick.

This map of the seafloor shows the Galápagos spreading center, a portion of the mid-ocean ridge in the Pacific Ocean, roughly 600 miles (1,000 km) west of South America. The dark blue areas reveal the deepest part of the rift. Red areas are the shallowest.

The Ultimate Hike

The Appalachian Trail is a 2,167-mile (3,489-kilometer) footpath that follows the ridge-line of the Appalachian Mountains from Maine to Georgia. Generally it takes five to seven months to hike from one end of the trail to the other. If it were possible to hike the mid-ocean ridge, walking at the same pace it takes to traverse the Appalachian Trail, a hiker would need eight to eleven years to complete the trek.

An aerial view of the Great Smoky Mountains, a part of the Appalachian Mountain chain running through Tennessee and North Carolina

The discovery of the mid-ocean ridge and deep-sea trenches came too late to prevent the German scientist Alfred Wegener from becoming an object of ridicule among other scientists. Wegener had been intrigued by the distribution of the continents and mountains on Earth's surface. He noticed that the coastlines of the continents on opposite sides of the Atlantic matched up like jigsaw pieces.

A sonar image of the rift valley bisecting the mid-Atlantic ridge

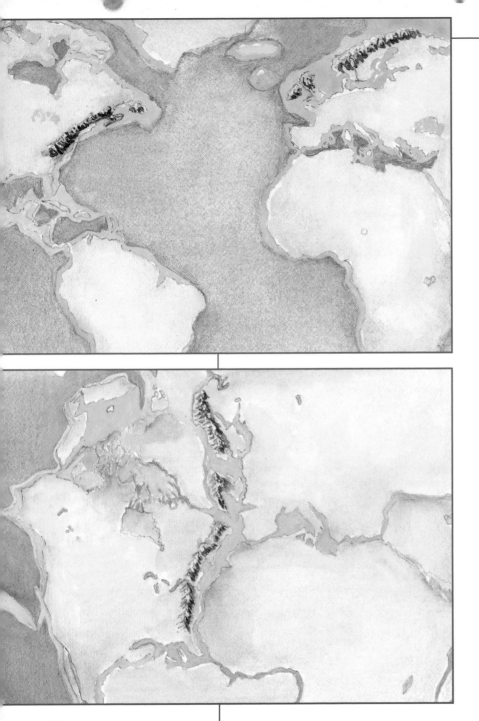

CLUES FOR CONTINENTAL DRIFT

South Africa enjoys a sunny and mild climate. However, deep scratches in South African rocks provided proof that South Africa once nestled closer to the South Pole and was covered by a thick ice sheet. Wegener used climate clues, such as these rock scars, to show that the position of continents had changed over time.

(Left) If you could close up the Atlantic Ocean, the continents of North and South America would fit together with the continents of Europe and Africa. (In fact, if the matching occurred along the borders of the continental shelves, not along the present-day coastlines of the continents, the fit would be nearly perfect.) The Appalachian Mountain chain along the east coast of America would form a single chain with the mountains of the British Isles and Scandinavia. Coal deposits in South Africa would line up with identical deposits in Brazil. All these matches supported Wegener's theory.

(above) Wegener bolstered his claim with fossil evidence. Fossils of Mesosaurus, a small aquatic lizard that lived about 280 million years ago, have been found only in Brazil and South Africa. If Mesosaurus had been capable of swimming across the ocean, its fossils would be more widespread. Wegener reasoned that Mesosaurus lived at a time when the South American and African continents were joined.

In 1912, Wegener proposed that all the continents had been united 300 million years ago in a single landmass, a supercontinent called Pangaea. According to Wegener the landmasses slowly broke apart. Over tens of millions of years, the pieces drifted through the oceans to their present-day locations, becoming the continents in existence today. This idea became known as the theory of continental drift.

In Wegener's time, most geologists believed that the Earth was slowly cooling, shrinking, and wrinkling. According to this concept, the continents were anchored in place and mountain ranges popped up where the crust shriveled like the skin of a dried-up apple. Wegener believed that if this were true, then mountains should be evenly sprinkled over the Earth's surface. But he found that *most* mountains cluster in narrow belts along the borders of continents.

Wegener claimed that mountains formed when continents collided and their edges crumpled. He gathered evidence from fossils, climate data, and landform features to support his argument. However, Wegener could not satisfactorily account for a force powerful enough to move continents. Most of his peers opposed his theory, some quite openly, and the notion of continental drift was largely ignored for the next 50 years.

By 1960, Wegener's theory could no longer be discarded. Harry Hess, an American geologist who initially had been baffled by the presence of trenches and the mid-ocean ridge, realized he had found the mechanism for continental drift-seafloor spreading. He suggested the radical idea that ocean floors moved like conveyor belts, hauling the continents along with them. According to Hess, the process starts at the mid-ocean ridge. There, volcanoes funnel hot magma—molten rock—from beneath Earth's crust up through the rift. The molten rock spreads out and forms a strip of solid rock along the center of the ridge as it hardens. More molten rock spurts up, splices the new rock in two, and pushes it out along both sides of the valley. This process gives birth to new seafloor.

The new seafloor slides away from the rift on both sides, like the belts of two treadmills moving in opposite directions. The seafloor cools, shrinks, and becomes denser. As it becomes denser it sinks lower into the hotter, softer rock beneath.

Consequently, older parts of the seafloor lie at greater depths than younger sections. Eventually the old seafloor disappears into a trench where it is recycled into the hot molten rock below. The entire process, from the birth of seafloor at the mid-ocean ridge to its destruction in a trench, might take about 200 million years. In the Pacific Ocean, trenches swallow the seafloor at a faster rate than the mid-ocean ridge spits it out. So the Pacific Ocean is shrinking. The Atlantic Ocean, which contains fewer trenches, is growing.

Shake, Rattle, and Roll

Records of seismic waves (ground vibrations produced by earthquakes) provided additional support for the existence of seafloor spreading. Most earthquakes begin in Earth's crust, where unstoppable forces squeeze the rock or pull it up, down, or sideways. Somewhat elastic, the rock responds to the stress by slowly changing shape and volume. When the strain becomes too great, the rock tears apart along a fault—a break in the crust. The rupture releases huge amounts of energy in the form of seismic waves that race out in all directions, trembling and shaking the ground. Instruments called seismographs record the ground motions created by seismic waves. The data allows scientists to pinpoint the origin and strength of an earthquake. Extensive earthquake data showed that these earthquakes frequently shake the mid-ocean ridge and trenches. Scientists deduced that these earthquakes announce the birth of new seafloor and the death of the old.

Evidence from Magnetic Memory

Compelling evidence for seafloor spreading came from an unexpected source— the magnetic properties of rock on the seafloor. Geologists have long been aware that the Earth is surrounded by a magnetic field and acts like a giant magnet. The magnetic force is strongest at the magnetic poles, which lie near the geographic North and South Poles. Although the force lines are invisible to humans, you can observe the effects of the magnetic field with a compass. The compass needle's north-seeking end will turn toward Earth's magnetic north.

The field however can flip-flop. The next time it happens, north-seeking compass

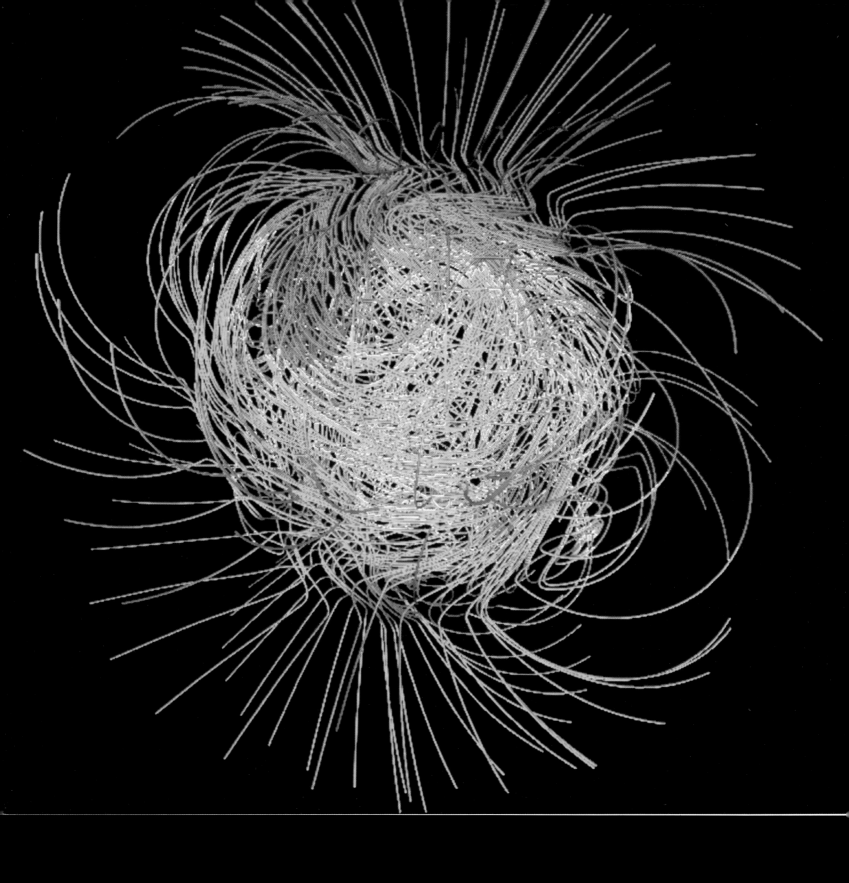

needles will point south. Magnetic reversals occur at irregular intervals. Sometimes half a million years or more may pass between them. At other times the intervals may be much shorter, less than 100,000 years. If the magnetic field began to reverse during your lifetime (which is unlikely), it would take 1,000 years or more to complete the process.

The seafloor provides a record of past magnetic reversals. The molten rock that forms the seafloor at the mid-ocean ridge contains iron bits. As the rock cools, the iron bits become oriented with the magnetic field. They align themselves with Earth's magnetic poles, just like a compass needle. By the time the rocks solidify completely, the iron bits are locked into place, giving the rock a magnetic memory.

Magnetometers—instruments that measure the strength and direction of magnetism—revealed that rocks on the seafloor are magnetized in a striped pattern. Long ribbons of rock that formed when Earth's magnetic field was what we consider normal alternate with ribbons of rock that formed when the field was reversed. The ribbons vary in width and lie parallel to the mid-ocean ridge. The pattern of stripes on one side of the ridge mirrors the pattern on the other. This could happen only if the matching ribbons formed at the same time.

The Source of Earth's Magnetic Field

If you could ride an elevator down to the center of the Earth, you would pass through four major layers—the crust, mantle, outer core, and inner core. The deeper you went, the hotter your surroundings would become and the greater the pressure. The heat arises partly from the decay of radioactive elements within the Earth and partly from the heat left over from the birth of the planet.

The innermost layer, the inner core, is solid and consists mainly of iron and some nickel. About one-third the size of the Moon, the inner core is a gigantic metal ball that spins freely inside Earth. Wrapped around the inner core is the outer core, a restless sea of molten metal. Swirling currents in the outer core spin the inner core. The inner and outer cores together create the Earth's magnetic field, turning the entire planet into an enormous bar magnet.

This illustration shows the magnetic field that surrounds Earth. The magnetic force is strongest at the magnetic poles, which are near the geographic North and South Poles.

35

EVIDENCE FROM DEEP-SEA DRILLING

Indisputable proof of seafloor spreading came from cores—samples of sediments and rocks gathered by drilling holes in the ocean bottom. In 1968, the research vessel *Glomar Challenger* began to collect cores. The *Glomar Challenger* looked like a cargo ship with an oil derrick plopped down on its deck. This was no coincidence. The design of the ship's drilling mechanism had been adapted from technology used for offshore oil exploration. The *Glomar Challenger* could send drilling pipes through water up to 20,000 feet (6 kilometers) deep. The drilling pipe was lowered through the "moon pool," a wide hole beneath the derrick through the ship's center. Once the drilling pipe reached the ocean bottom, its sharp cutting end could bore an additional 2,500 feet (750 meters) into the sediments and rocks. As the pipe worked its way down, it filled with seafloor material. A steel cable passed through the drilling pipe retrieved the long cylinders of sediments and rocks. These cores were about 30 feet (9 meters) in length and 8 inches (20 centimeters) around.

Like the pages of a calendar, the sediment and rock layers within each core measured the passage of time. Fossilized remains of marine organisms locked within the sediments provided a means of interpreting the calendar. Fossil studies have shown that during the past 3.5 billion years, myriad species of organisms have appeared on Earth, have thrived for millions of years, and then have become extinct or evolved into distinctly different kinds of organisms. Researchers use "index fossils" to determine the approximate age of a seafloor layer. Index fossils come from organisms that appeared for only a short time span in Earth's history but were geographically widespread. Knowing the time period in which a particular fossilized life-form existed enables scientists to date similar fossils.

Index fossils do not give the exact age of a rock layer. To get a more precise age, researchers use a technique called absolute dating. Rock contains radioactive elements—unstable elements that decay (breakdown) into other elements at constant rates. For example, radioactive potassium-40 breaks down into the more stable element argon-40. The half-life of radioactive potassium-40—the time it takes for half of the element to decay—is 1,310 million years. The age of a rock can be determined by comparing the amount of the radioactive "parent" element

The drilling derrick on the deck of the *Glomar Challenger* straddles an opening to the sea called a moon pool.

(like potassium-40) to the amount of stable "daughter" elements (like argon-40) in it. Absolute dating is especially useful when no fossils are present in a rock.

Using a variety of dating techniques, researchers aboard the *Glomar Challenger* determined that the youngest seafloor rocks were always found closest to the ridge. The older rocks were inevitably located the farthest away. Interestingly, the age of the most ancient seafloor rocks—180 million years—paled in comparison to the age of the oldest continental rocks, which are nearly 4 billion years old.

In 1983, the *Glomar Challenger* was retired. Two years later it was replaced by a newer ship which could drill deeper—the *JOIDES Resolution* (Joint Oceanographic Institutions for Deep Earth Sampling).

BURSTING AT THE SEAMS

The evidence in support of seafloor spreading led to the development of the theory of plate tectonics. According to this theory, Earth's hard outer surface is broken into about a dozen gigantic rocky slabs called tectonic plates. The plates fit tightly together like the pieces of a cracked eggshell. Unlike the pieces of eggshell, however, the plates move slowly relative to one another. They are pushed and pulled by the gradual flow of hotter and softer rock beneath them. Traveling at rates generally between 1 and 6 inches (2.5 and 15 centimeters) per year, the roving plates carry whatever lies on top of them: the continents, islands, ocean floor—even you.

Where plates scrape sideways past each other, their rugged borders jam together and build up tremendous stress. Eventually the plates lunge past each other, triggering colossal earthquakes. This is happening along the San Andreas Fault, the boundary of the North American plate, which carries most of North America and part of the Atlantic Ocean, and the Pacific plate, which transports nearly all the Pacific Ocean and a sliver of California.

Where two plates toting continents collide, they squeeze Earth's hard outer surface, twisting the rocks and punching up jagged mountains. The

Trilobite fossils date back more than 500 million years and are used as index fossils.

impact of India crashing into Eurasia produced the Himalayan Mountains. Although this mountain building started 50 million years ago, it still continues, lifting the Himalayas to even loftier heights. The upheavals of land caused by colliding continents generate immense earthquakes, including one that struck Tangshan, China, in 1976, killing hundreds of thousands of people.

When a plate carting a continent careens into one lugging seafloor, a deep-sea trench develops. In fits and starts, the plate with the seafloor slips beneath the continent and melts into the hotter, softer rock beneath. This process formed the Aleutian Trench, an underwater gorge just off the Alaskan coast. The trench extends 2,300 miles (3,700 kilometers) from Kodiak Island to the tip of the Aleutian Island chain. There the Pacific Ocean floor is being forced underneath the North American continent.

Trenches also appear when two plates carrying ocean floor plow into each other. The one hauling older, heavier seafloor bends and dives beneath the other. This warping process created the Mariana Trench.

The death of seafloor is violent. The clashing plates snag each other like Velcro strips, unleashing earthquakes when they wrench free. Additionally the descending plate heats up and partially melts the plate above it. The resulting molten rock may give rise to a string of volcanoes that blast through the overriding plate.

The summit of Mount Saint Elias in Alaska

41

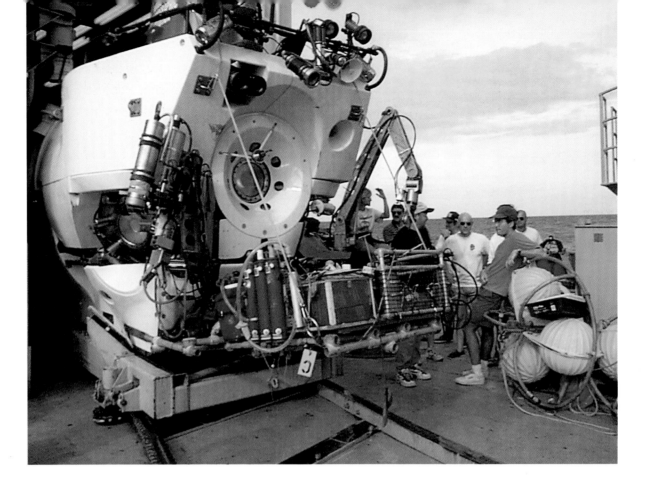

The submersible *Alvin* on the deck of its mother ship

When two plates split apart, a rift marks their boundary. Most diverging boundaries are found underwater along the mid-ocean ridge. The Earth literally bursts at the seams along the ridge as the plates rip apart. However, it was not until the early 1970s and the development of submersibles strong enough to resist the crush of the deep that humans directly observed the volcanic by-products of this phenomenon on the seafloor.

Submersibles are small submarines with thick metal walls built to withstand immense pressure. Thrusters—propellers that expel a stream of water—allow pilots to maneuver submersibles. Designed primarily for scientific research, submersibles can dive much deeper than submarines constructed for warfare. The best-known submersible, *Alvin*, was built in 1964 as a joint project between the U.S. Navy and the Woods Hole Oceanographic Institution on Cape Cod, Massachusetts. One of *Alvin*'s most successful voyages occurred 10 years later during Project FAMOUS (French-American Mid-Ocean Undersea Study), an expedition of French and American scientists. Part adventurer, part scientist, these researchers were devoted to making the first direct observation of seafloor spreading. While exploring the mid-Atlantic ridge, 400 miles (640 kilometers) southwest of the Azores Islands, the team aboard *Alvin* spotted a bizarre landscape nearly 2 miles (3.2 kilometers) below the surface. Fresh lava shaped like fluffy pillows, broken bubbles, and large haystacks covered the seafloor. In some places the lava resembled toothpaste squeezed out in long twisting tubes. The newly minted rock provided unmistakable proof that seafloor spreading was an ongoing process.

Pillow lava

Alvin

When *Alvin* was launched in 1964, it was equipped with a steel sphere with space for two people and it could dive only as deep as 6,000 feet (1,830 meters). In 1973, the submersible was refitted with a titanium sphere that could hold three people. Lighter and stronger than the steel sphere, the titanium one made it possible for *Alvin* to dive more than twice as deep as originally designed. Additional upgrades extended *Alvin's* maximum depth to 14,700 feet (4,500 meters). The deepest-diving submersible is the *Shinkai 6500*, which was built in Japan in 1989. It can reach 21,320 feet (6,500 meters).

Alvin's three tiny portholes provide the crew with a view of the outside. The submersible's powerful searchlights can illuminate an area up to 40 feet (12 meters) in each direction. Still and video cameras make visual records of the scene for examination later. *Alvin* is equipped with a manipulator arm on each side to collect samples of rocks, sediments, and sea animals for study at the surface.

It takes two hours for the submersible to descend. Powered by batteries, it cruises between .5 and 2 nautical miles (3,000 and 12,000 feet or 900 and 3,700 meters) per hour and can stay underwater up to 10 hours under normal conditions. Operated by the Woods Hole Oceanographic Institution, *Alvin* undertakes 150 to 200 dives a year.

Alvin exploring the seafloor

45

chapter 3

UNDERSEA FINDS

In 1966, a U.S. Air Force B-52 bomber collided with another aircraft over the Mediterranean Sea. The wreckage was scattered over a 10-square-mile (26-square-kilometer) area on land and sea along the Spanish coast. Among the debris were four hydrogen bombs that had parachuted to the surface. Each H-bomb was capable of destroying much of Spain and Portugal, as well as part of North Africa. Authorities recovered three of the bombs on land but the fourth had plummeted to the sea bottom. A navy spokesperson compared the likelihood of finding the bomb to trying to find the eye of a needle in a field of haystacks in the dark. Nevertheless American officials feared that the Soviets, America's Cold War rivals, would retrieve it. (The Cold War was a rivalry between the United States and the Union of Soviet Socialist Republics that resulted in the buildup of weapons of mass destruction on both sides. The hostilities lasted from 1945 to 1991 and threatened to plunge the world into a nuclear war.)

To locate the missing weapon, the U.S. Navy brought in *Alvin* and another submersible. At first the submersible crews didn't know what to look for. The H-bomb was such a topsecret weapon that the navy refused to release a description of it. Eventually, however, a practical-minded individual showed the pilots a photograph of the bomb without the permission of the navy.

On *Alvin*'s tenth dive, the crew spotted the billowing parachute with the lost bomb attached to it. But they could not retrieve the 12,800-pound (5,800-kilogram) weapon. For the actual recovery the navy used its newest ROV, called CURV (Cable-controlled Underwater Research Vessel). *CURV* looked like a sled equipped with lights, cameras, and a gigantic claw-shaped manipulator arm. During the rescue attempt, *CURV* became hopelessly entangled in the parachute. When the ROV was hauled back to the surface, it fortuitously brought the parachute and bomb along with it.

Alvin's manipulator arm reaches toward a black-smoker chimney in the east Pacific rise.

GEYSERS ON THE OCEAN BOTTOM

Alvin's role in locating the missing H-bomb wasn't its greatest accomplishment. In 1977, geologists aboard the submersible made the most exciting undersea discovery of all time. And it challenged the commonly held belief that all life-forms depend on sunlight and photosynthesis. The scientists were exploring the mid-ocean ridge near the Galápagos Islands, at a depth of 8,000 feet (2,400 kilometers). To their astonishment, *Alvin's* outside lights revealed a riot of life: mussel reefs, gardens of tube worms, fields of Frisbee-size clams, pink fish, blind crabs, and other odd-looking creatures never encountered before. How could such an oasis of life flourish there? This ecosystem was situated far too deep for the Sun's rays to reach. And the drizzle of "marine snow"—bits of dead organisms and waste material that drift down from higher levels of the ocean—could not support so many organisms.

The bizarre animals were clustered around hot undersea geysers—hydrothermal vents—that were erupting on the ocean bottom. Life near a hydrothermal vent does not draw its energy from sunlight and photosynthesis. It relies on chemosynthesis, the use of chemical energy to make simple sugars from carbon dioxide and water. Vent water is rich in foul-smelling hydrogen sulfide gas. Bacteria harness the chemical energy stored in sulfides for chemosynthesis. The bacteria, in turn, become a banquet for the strange creatures. Some vent animals eat the bacteria directly—filtering them from the water or scraping them off rocks. The giant tube worm, however, has no mouth or digestive system. Instead it developed a symbiotic relationship with the bacteria (a relationship in which both organisms benefit). A tube worm houses billions of bacteria in spongy tissue within its body and brings sulfides to them via its bloodstream. The bacteria convert the sulfides into food and provide nutrition for the tube worm.

You harbor "aliens" inside your body, too. Each of your cells contains mitochondria—mini-energy factories—that convert sugar into energy for the cell to use. All plant, animal, and fungus cells have them. Mitochondria contain their own DNA—genetic material—and they are about the same size as bacteria. During evolution an ancestral cell common to all plants, animals, and fungi may have captured a bacterial cell and formed an alliance with it. In exchange for a steady

supply of sugar, the bacterium took on the role of the cell's powerhouse. This arrangement was passed along every time the cell reproduced. It then made its way up the evolutionary ladder as higher forms of life appeared.

COLD SEEPS

In 1984, *Alvin* made possible another spectacular discovery. While exploring the depths of the Gulf of Mexico, researchers aboard *Alvin* stumbled across a profusion of deep-sea creatures nearly identical to those found in vent communities. Tube worms, mussels, clams, and other exotic creatures dependent on chemical-eating bacteria abounded. However, these organisms flourished in cold water near the continental margin, far from the hot hydrothermal vents on the mid-ocean ridge. These bacteria obtained their energy from cold seeps—places where water rich in sulfides or methane (better known as natural gas) oozes from the seafloor. Some cold seeps are "puddles" on the ocean bottom, five times saltier than the surrounding water. Cold seeps are the same temperature as the nearly freezing water around them.

The origin of cold seeps can be traced back to tiny plants and animals that once thrived in shallow ancient seas. When the organisms died, their remains dropped to the ocean bottom and were covered by layers of mud, sand, and other sediments. Over time the weight of the top layers squeezed the bottom ones, compacting them. Gradually the sediments were transformed into rocks such as sandstone and shale. The remains changed into crude oil and natural gas.

The oil and gas rose through tiny holes in the porous overlying rock. In some places denser rock blocked their escape. Like water filling the spaces of a sponge, trapped oil and gas filled the holes in the porous rock. Today much of the world's oil and gas deposits are locked in the thick seafloor sediments skirting the continents. Cold seeps appear where bubbles of gas and blobs of oil escape through cracks in the rock and stream up to the seabed. Methane ice forms when natural gas seeps through the seafloor and becomes trapped in a framework of water ice crystals.

In addition to the Gulf of Mexico, cold seeps have also been explored along the Japanese coast and the west coast of North America in places where one tec-

TUBE WORMS
AND OTHER VENT ANIMALS

(Left) A giant tube worm looks like a long white garden hose with a slender blood-red tulip protruding from the end. Tube worms can grow as tall as 12 feet (3.7 m), more than twice the height of the average adult human. Hemoglobin, the same molecule that colors your blood bright red, gives a tube worm plume its crimson hue.

(Top Right) Blind white crabs are often the top predator in vent communities.

(Upper Right) The Pompeii worm, the most heat-loving animal known, thrives in vent water as hot as 176°F (80°C). To put this in perspective, a comfortable room temperature for people is 72°F (22°C), more than 100°F (38°C) cooler.

(Lower Right) Deep-sea dandelions are about the size of golf balls. Although they superficially resemble a dandelion plant gone to seed, there is nothing flowerlike about them. Deep-sea dandelions are jellies, complete with soft bodies and stinging tentacles. A close cousin of the Portuguese man-of-war, the deep-sea dandelion is a colony of individual animals that support each other.

(Bottom Right) The survival of mussels at hydrothermal vents is linked to the sulfur-eating bacteria that the mussels host in their gills.

tonic plate dips beneath another and forms a deep-sea trench. At the boundary of the plates, the energy-rich fluids are squeezed out of the mud and sediments like water wrung from a washcloth.

THE CHEMICALS OF LIFE

No one knows how life began on Earth, but some scientists believe that hydrothermal vents provided the chemicals necessary for it to arise. According to one theory, a community of one-celled organisms originated in hydrothermal vents about 3.8 billion years ago. These microorganisms became the ancestors of all living things.

You probably know that all organisms (except for viruses) are made of the same basic building blocks—cells. A cell is the smallest unit that can survive independently and reproduce itself. Living things range in size from simple one-celled organisms like bacteria, to highly complex organisms like you, composed of trillions of cells.

Cells, in turn, consist of chemicals. Water is the major component—it makes up about 65 percent of a cell. Different kinds of organisms have different "recipes" of chemicals that they need to survive. They obtain these chemicals by stealing them from the environment or by gobbling up other organisms. You get most of the chemicals you need from the food you eat and drink. With every breath you take, you extract the oxygen you must have from the air. Likewise organisms that live in the sea take everything they need from their surroundings.

Coral reefs are home to some of the ocean's most wondrous creatures. They were built by billions of corals, tiny jellylike animals with hard shells made of calcite. Corals extract calcium directly from seawater and use it to make calcite. Corals live in large groups fastened to each other by their calcite shells. When

A colorful coral reef in the Philippines

52

THE ULTIMATE METAL EXTRACTORS

(Left) Copper is barely detectable in ocean water but lobsters, clams, octopuses, and crabs—like this Sally Lightfoot—need it in order to live. Instead of iron in their blood to carry oxygen, they have copper, which colors their blood blue.

(Top) Sea squirts have high concentrations of the metal vanadium in their blood. The high levels of vanadium may be a defense against predators, as large concentrations of vanadium are toxic to most animals.

(Right) Lobsters make use of cobalt in their shells, but normally cobalt's blue coloring is not visible. About 1 in every 2 million lobsters has a blue shell.

corals die, their shells remain in place and new corals make their homes on top of them. Over thousands of years this process results in reefs that may be hundreds of miles long.

What do you have in common with a coral? You are a calcium extractor, too. Healthy adult women have about 2 pounds (.9 kilogram) of calcium in their bodies, while men have about 2.5 to 3 pounds (1.1 to 1.4 kilograms). Practically 99 percent of this calcium is found in our bones and teeth. Without calcium, you would be toothless and as limp as a jelly.

Your body also contains significant amounts of phosphorus, magnesium, potassium, sulfur, sodium, and chlorine. An adult body has about 1 teaspoon's (5 milliliters') worth of iron. Most of it is found in hemoglobin molecules inside red blood cells, where it serves as an oxygen carrier and gives blood its red color.

The human body contains traces of copper, zinc, iodine, and cobalt. They appear in such small quantities that scientists measure them in milligrams and micrograms. To get a handle on how small these measurements are, imagine a paper clip. A paper clip weighs 1 gram. Now divide that paper clip by 1,000. The weight of one-thousandth of a paper clip is 1 milligram. If you divide the paper clip by 1 million, one-millionth of a paper clip equals 1 microgram.

Small as these amounts are, they are critical to our well-being. For example, a typical adult man has approximately 30 milligrams of iodine in his body. An iodine deficiency causes goiter—an enlargement of the thyroid gland. If a pregnant woman lacks iodine, her child will be born with cretinism, a disease that causes permanent mental retardation. In the United States and Canada, iodine is readily available in fish, shellfish, and iodized salt (salt that has had iodine added to it). However, iodine deficiency is a problem in inland regions of underdeveloped countries in Asia, Africa, and South America.

DOES LIFE EXIST BEYOND EARTH?

Europa, the fourth largest of Jupiter's 16 moons, may have the conditions necessary for life to exist. Pictures from the *Galileo* spacecraft reveal that a thick layer of ice covers Europa. In places the ice appears to have broken up, moved apart, and then re-formed. Water pushing up from below could have caused the ice to shift. Scientists speculate that an ocean of water heated by hydrothermal vents may lie beneath Europa's ice. Where there is water, life may exist.

If life exists beyond our planet, it will be interesting to learn how the organisms obtain their nutrition. Will their food chains be based on predator-prey relationships—resulting in the natural killers so prevalent on Earth? Or will the organisms have symbiotic relationships with energy-capturing producers housed within their tissues? Perhaps they will have totally different mechanisms that have not evolved on Earth.

chapter 4

MINERAL RICHES

Imagine a cave big enough to hold two large city buses standing on end. Then line the walls, floor, and ceiling with chunks of pure gold. Such a cave once existed in an extinct volcano. In 1914, miners uncovered the cave inside the Cresson gold mine in Cripple Creek, Colorado. The gold-studded chamber was the interior of a giant geode—a rounded hollow rock. In four weeks, miners removed more than $25 million worth of gold at today's prices.

If you dug for gold in your backyard, you would be quite disappointed. Gold and other metals are not evenly distributed throughout the Earth's crust. If they were, most would appear in such small quantities that they would be impossible to extract. Volcanoes are responsible for concentrating much of the metals found on the Earth's surface. Hydrothermal vents play a key role in this process.

Most hydrothermal vents emerge along the rifts of the mid-ocean ridge. As you know, this is where volcanoes belch out lava that hardens into new rocky seafloor. As the fresh lava cools, it cracks, permitting ice-cold seawater to seep into the molten rock below. The descending water is heated far above 212 degrees Fahrenheit (100 degrees Celsius), the boiling point at sea level. However, the superheated water remains a liquid. The enormous pressure created by the weight of the overlying ocean prevents it from boiling. The superheated water dissolves minerals from the surrounding rock in the same way that hot tea dissolves sugar. Some of the dissolved minerals contain metals, such as gold, silver, copper, zinc, lead, and iron. The resulting mineral-rich "broth" is technically known as a *solution*—a mixture in which one substance is dissolved inside another.

The scalding-hot brew rises quickly and spews out of seafloor vents like water blasting from a fire hose. When the solution hits the frigid ocean water, some of the dissolved minerals precipitate, or separate out. They change into solid

These selenite crystals were discovered in 2001 in two adjacent caves within a silver and zinc mine in Chihuahua, Mexico. They are the largest natural crystals in the world and are located 1,200 feet (370 m) below the surface, where temperatures reach 150 degrees Fahrenheit (65°C).

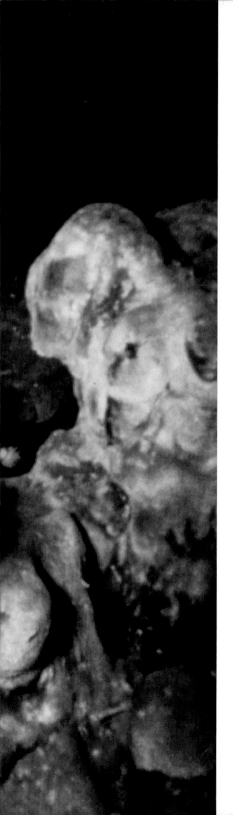

particles, giving the gushing water the appearance of smoke. Consequently researchers nicknamed the vents "smokers."

White smokers billow out milky-colored water with temperatures ranging from 392 to 626 degrees Fahrenheit (200 to 330 degrees Celsius). They contain light-colored minerals. Black smokers produce even hotter plumes, as high as 750 degrees Fahrenheit (400 degrees Celsius). The plumes contain dark-colored minerals. Nothing can live where water temperatures soar so high. Vent animals inhabit the cooler water nearby where the vent water mixes rapidly with chilly seawater.

Undersea vents build up immense mounds, or chimneys, around their openings. The tallest chimney discovered so far is Poseidon, a 180-foot (55-meter) vent in the "Lost City," a hydrothermal field with the largest vents ever found. The Lost City is located on the Atlantis Massif, an undersea mountain in the mid-Atlantic. It was found in the year 2000 during a routine seafloor mapping project. Unlike other hydrothermal vents, the ones in the Lost City lack sulfides and they spew fluid rich in carbonate—the same material that forms limestone. As a result the chimneys are light in color.

The seafloor beneath the Lost City is 1.5 million years old and lies far from any volcanic activity. Apparently the heat that "powers" the vents is generated by a chemical change. When ocean water seeps through deep cracks in the seafloor there, it comes into contact with rocks containing

A white smoker on the Pacific Ocean floor

"Saracen's Head" is a black smoker found in the mid-Atlantic ridge.

the mineral olivine. The olivine reacts with the seawater and turns into the mineral serpentine. In the process, heat is released.

Some hydrothermal vent sites have become wondrous storehouses of mineral wealth, with metal deposits worth billions of dollars. As the ocean floor moves away from the mid-ocean ridge, the vents lose their heat source and fizzle out. The animal life they support dies out, too. However, the mineral deposits remain and tag along for the ride. When the seafloor is ultimately consumed in a deep-sea trench, the overriding plate acts like a bulldozer blade. It skims off the top layer of the sinking seafloor. In the process, it thrusts some of the mineral deposits, seashells, and other rubble on the ocean floor onto the overriding plate. In time, the jostling of tectonic plates may raise these deposits above sea level.

However, the sinking plate carries the bulk of the mineral wealth into the trench. As the sinking plate heats up it produces magma, which feeds the volcanoes on the overriding plate. The minerals melt and become part of the magma. The volcanoes re-create the conditions that brought the minerals to the seafloor. Only this time groundwater—not hot, salty seawater—circulates in the cracked rock. The groundwater heats up when it nears the magma and dissolves some of the minerals.

The mineral-rich water rises into the cracks in the solid rock above, where it cools. The minerals precipitate out crystal by crystal, sometimes in the form of pure metals such as silver or gold. Over long periods of time, the metals become concentrated in the Earth's crust and form rich deposits called veins. These veins are part of the solid rock inside mountains, which formed near subduction zones, places where one plate sank beneath another. The rich gold deposits that triggered gold rushes in California and Alaska were created in this way.

Although volcanoes concentrate metals, they do not create them. Metals are born in the center of massive stars. The extreme heat and pressure in a star's core generate fusion reactions. In a fusion reaction, lighter elements such as silicon and oxygen join to produce heavier elements such as iron and nickel. During a supernova—the explosive death of a massive star—the metals and other components of the star are flung into space where they may become the raw materials of new solar systems. The calcium, iron, magnesium, potassium, sodium, and other metals in your body were all created in stars.

This artist's conception of a supernova was drawn on a computer.

Minerals Formed by Evaporation

If you have ever swum in the ocean, you may have noticed salt crystals on your skin after the seawater evaporated. Similarly when ancient seas dried up, they left minerals behind, including abundant deposits of halite—common table salt. In the United States, halite deposits can be found in the Midwest, Southwest, and in "salt domes" buried more than 2 miles (3.2 kilometers) below the seabed of the Gulf of Mexico. Salt domes make effective oil traps. Other mineral treasures left behind by seawater evaporation include gypsum, the chief ingredient of plaster, and potassium-containing minerals, which are used in fertilizers.

MANGANESE NODULES

Scattered across vast segments of the deep-ocean floor are manganese nodules—dark lumps of metal rich in manganese and iron. They also contain significant amounts of copper, nickel, and cobalt. The nodules seem to have more in common with pearls than with metal deposits created by volcanoes. Pearls form on the inside of an oyster shell when a grain of sand or a tiny parasite enters the shell. The oyster coats the intruder with a slimy substance that hardens into a thin pearly layer. Over the course of several years, the oyster gradually adds more layers until the invader is totally encased in a pearl.

A sand grain, a shell fragment, or even a shark's tooth may form the core of a developing manganese nodule. The metals precipitate out of seawater and accumulate in thin layers around the core. Nodule growth is incredibly slow—.04 to .4 inches (1 to 10 millimeters) per million years. Someday the manganese nodules may be worth a fortune. So far, the high cost of seafloor mining, disputes among nations over mineral rights, and the relatively low price paid for metals have slowed commercial mining ventures.

THE RACE TO CONQUER "INNER SPACE"

Many countries are aggressively developing strategies to master the watery realm. The Japanese submersible *Shinkai 6500*, the French submersibles *Nautile* and *Victor*, and the *Russian Mir I* and *Mir II* can all achieve depths of 3.7 miles (6 kilometers). These manned vehicles can dive at least .9 mile (1.5 kilometers) deeper than *Alvin* and can access 35 percent more of the ocean floor. Consequently they can explore most of the ocean bottom except the deepest trenches.

The international race is on to locate the richest undersea mineral resources and offshore oil reserves. But there are other "prizes," too. Marine biologists are eager to find marine organisms that may produce new medicines that might lead to a cure for cancer or other diseases. Climate experts seek clues to short-term and long-term climate changes. Geologists from earthquake-prone Japan are studying trenches to determine whether warning signs are given prior to a major quake. And of course, archeological treasures abound. Not only are there sunken ships to be explored, but occasionally in shallow coastal areas an ancient city—such as Hērákleion along the Egyptian coast—is uncovered.

What makes a submersible such an appealing tool for working in the deep ocean—its human cargo—is also its major drawback. The safety risk, high cost, and time needed to carry out just one mission limit a submersible's usefulness. So ROVs equipped with sonar and cameras have become the workhorses of undersea scientific and commercial operations. Safer, more versatile, and less costly to operate, they have been used to lay undersea cables and maintain offshore drilling equipment used by the oil industry.

In 2002, the most sophisticated American ROV, *Jason II*, was introduced. Able to achieve depths of 21,320 feet (6,500 meters), it has better environmental sensors, increased maneuverability, and can collect more samples than its predecessors. It can also communicate on the Internet. However, like all ROVs, it still requires a mother ship and a crew to monitor and guide its activities.

HUNTING THE *TITANIC*

Dr. Robert Ballard made use of both a submersible and ROV technology during his search for the *Titanic*. Dr. Ballard is an American geologist who has explored more of the deep ocean than any other adventurer. He was one of the Project FAMOUS scientists aboard *Alvin*, who discovered "toothpaste lava" and other evidence of seafloor spreading along the mid-ocean ridge. Nine years later in 1985, Ballard participated in another expedition with French researchers—the hunt for the wreck of the ship *Titanic*.

SUBMERSIBLES

(Left) The French submersible *Nautile*

(Top) *Mir II*, a Russian submersible, hovers over the ruins of the Titanic.

(Bottom) The *Johnson Sea-Link* submersible can dive to a depth of about 3,000 feet (1 km).

Launched in 1912, the *Titanic* was the largest and most luxurious ocean liner of her day. The ship was considered unsinkable. But on its very first voyage, a transatlantic crossing from Southampton, England, to New York City, the *Titanic* sideswiped an iceberg. The collision ripped out rivets holding the ship's hull frame together. Water poured through the open seams, flooding the *Titanic*. An estimated 1,513 people perished and another 705 survived. The ship plunged beneath 12,500 feet (4,000 meters) of water, 1,000 miles (1,600 kilometers) east of Boston, Massachusetts.

The French-American quest to find the *Titanic*'s grave began in July 1985. Scientists aboard the French research vessel *Le Suroit* started by slowly towing a side-scan sonar device back and forth over the search area. Day after day, the device produced monotonous images of flat mud-covered deep-sea floor, interrupted occasionally by images of rippled sand. Three weeks into the pursuit, Dr. Ballard and his group of American researchers arrived on the vessel *Knorr*. They brought along *Argo*, a remotely operated underwater sled equipped with a video camera and bright floodlights. Attached to the *Knorr* by a strong cable, *Argo* was lowered into the depths. Trawling within 50 feet (15 meters) of the ocean bottom, *Argo* sent back detailed images.

For nine long days researchers scrutinized the images, looking for any hint of debris from the *Titanic*. With only five days left in the expedition they were almost ready to admit defeat when *Argo* cruised into the history books. Stark images of rusted pipes, riveted hull plates, big boilers, and other twisted wreckage came into focus. Finally the stern section (the back half) of the ship appeared, resting upright. The *Titanic* had snapped in two before sinking. The stern and bow lay nearly 2,000 feet (600 meters) apart on the ocean floor. Scattered between the two main sections lay much debris.

The next summer Ballard returned to *Titanic*'s graveyard with *Alvin* and a crew from the Woods Hole Oceanographic Institution. Tethered to *Alvin* was *Jason Junior*, a small, highly maneuverable, camera-toting ROV. On the seafloor *Alvin*'s crew controlled *Jason Junior* as it inspected the *Titanic*'s interior, sending back eerie and astounding images. After 74 years underwater, little remained inside the ghost liner that reflected its original grandeur. "Rusticles"—veins of rust that resemble icicles—covered the ship. Wood-eating creatures had consumed the wooden decks. Ballard left the contents of the *Titanic* undisturbed as a memorial to its victims. But in later years, treasure hunters plundered the wreck.

Robert Ballard has explored other sunken wrecks, including the American aircraft carrier USS *Yorktown*, the ill-fated passenger liner *Lusitania*, the German battleship *Bismarck*, and ancient shipwrecks in the Mediterranean Sea. In 1989, Dr. Ballard founded the JASON Project, a program that brings the excitement of scientific discovery into the classroom via Internet or satellite technology. It allows students to communicate with scientists as they work in the depths of the ocean, in icy polar regions, or in other extreme environments. Students can also view images sent back by ROV as they are being photographed.

AUVs

Autonomous undersea vehicles (AUVs) may become a reasonable alternative to extending the reach of humans beneath the ocean. These undersea vehicles work independently—they carry no people and need no cables. Batteries or other long-lasting energy sources provide the power. Designed to carry out missions with preprogrammed instructions, AUVs require little human intervention.

The Autonomous Benthic Explorer (ABE) built by the Woods Hole Oceanographic Institution was one of the first AUVs put into operation. Programmed to survey the rugged seafloor, ABE can descend to a depth of 16,400 feet (5,000 meters) and remain underwater for weeks. At the end of each mission, a research vessel retrieves ABE after it surfaces and downloads its data.

By the beginning of the twenty-first century, at least 66 AUVs were being developed by at least 12 or more countries. One of the most promising of the new AUVs is the *Slocum Glider*, a diving robot introduced in 2002 by Webb Research Corporation of Falmouth, Massachusetts. This glider can remain at sea for up to five years, communicating with scientists via satellite. It moves at a slow speed, zigzagging up and down through the water by changing buoyancy (its tendency to float). The glider is designed to measure temperature and saltiness, map currents and eddies, count microscopic plants, and monitor whale communications.

A GHOSTLY TREASURE

Many objects from the *Titanic* remained intact, preserved in the near-freezing waters of the North Atlantic Ocean. These artifacts offer a rare opportunity for study of the deep ocean.

(Left) The prow of the sunken *Titanic*

(Top) Dishes from the *Titanic* are "stacked" horizontally on the sandy ocean bottom.

(Bottom) A remnant of one of the *Titanic*'s turbines—electric generators—lies on the seafloor.

Because of relatively low production costs—about $50,000 each—hundreds of these gliders may wind up in the ocean someday.

The exploration of the ocean's depths has just begun, and the tools to help with this task are still in their early childhood. So far, only a tiny fraction of the seafloor and the ocean's midwaters (3 to 4 miles or 5 to 6 kilometers down) have been investigated. For the adventurers of tomorrow, opportunity awaits. The potential to make new scientific and medical discoveries is enormous. Perhaps untapped mineral reserves on the seafloor could trigger gold rushes unrivaled by those that came before. And of course there are plenty of other shipwrecks with sunken treasure yet to be found. All these adventures and more await those daring enough to risk the dangers of the deep.

Glossary

ABYSSAL PLAIN—the vast flat region of the deep-sea floor

AUV—short for Autonomous Undersea Vehicle

CELL—the smallest organized unit of a living thing that can survive independently and reproduce itself

CHEMOSYNTHESIS—the process by which bacteria use chemical energy to manufacture their own food

COLD SEEP—a place on the ocean bottom where water rich in sulfides or methane oozes up through cracks in the seafloor

CONTINENTAL DRIFT—the theory that the continents slowly shift position

CONTINENTAL SHELF—the shallow sea closest to the continent

CONTINENTAL SLOPE—the steep incline separating the continental shelf from the deep ocean floor

EARTHQUAKE—the shaking that results from the movement of rock beneath the Earth's surface

ECOSYSTEM—all the living and nonliving things that interact in a specific area

HEMOGLOBIN—an iron-containing molecule that transports oxygen

HOLD—the inside of a ship below deck where cargo is usually stored

HULL—the frame of a ship

HURRICANE—a severe tropical storm that begins at sea with winds 74 miles (119 kilometers) per hour or more

HYDROTHERMAL VENTS—hot springs located on the ocean floor

ISTHMUS—a narrow piece of land that connects two larger land areas

LAVA—melted rock that flows out of a volcano

MAGMA—melted rock beneath the Earth's surface

MAGNETIC FIELD—the area around a magnet in which its force affects objects

Marine snow—the remains of dead organisms and waste material that drizzle down from higher levels of the ocean

Mid-ocean ridge—the undersea mountain chain

Nugget—a rock containing gold

Oozes—soft deposits of mud and the remains of plants and animals on the deep-sea floor

Photosynthesis—the process by which plants and plantlike organisms use light energy to make sugar and release oxygen

Pressure—the force pushing on an area or surface

Radioactive element—an unstable element that breaks down into other elements, releasing fast-moving particles and energy during the process

Rift valley—a deep canyon formed by separating tectonic plates

ROV—short for Remotely Operated Vehicle; an underwater robot

Seafloor spreading—the process by which new molten material is added to the ocean floor along the boundaries of spreading tectonic plates

Sediments—small solid particles that come from rocks or the remains of living things

Seismic wave—a vibration that moves through the Earth, carrying the energy released during an earthquake

Solution—a type of mixture in which one substance is dissolved in another

Sonar device—an instrument that uses sound waves to chart the oceans, track submarines, and hunt fish

Subduction—the process by which an oceanic plate sinks beneath another plate

Submersible—a small underwater vehicle with a thick metal hull that can withstand the extreme pressure of the deep ocean

Sulfide—a compound containing the element sulfur

Symbiotic relationship—a close connection between two different kinds of organisms in which both benefit

Tectonic plate—one of more than a dozen sections of the crust and part of the underlying mantle that moves independently

Trench—a deep canyon on the ocean floor where one tectonic plate overrides another

Volcano—a place where molten rock emerges through a weak spot in the Earth's crust

Books

Earle, Sylvia A. *Dive: My Adventures in the Deep Frontier.* Washington, D.C.: National Geographic Society, 1999.

Gowell, Elizabeth Tayntor. *Fountains of Life: The Story of Deep Sea Vents.* New York: Franklin Watts, 1998.

Kovacs, Deborah. *Dive to the Deep Ocean: Voyages of Exploration and Discovery.* Austin, TX: Raintree Steck-Vaughn, 2000.

Markle, Sandra. *Pioneering Ocean Depths.* New York: Atheneum, 1995.

Sullivan, George. *To the Bottom of the Sea: The Exploration of Exotic Life, the Titanic, and Other Secrets of the Oceans.* Brookfield, CT: Twenty-First Century Books, 1999.

Van Dover, Cindy Lee. *Deep-Ocean Journeys: Discovering New Life at the Bottom of the Sea.* Reading, MA: Addison-Wesley, 1996.

Web Sites

"Cold Seeps," Web site sponsored by the Department of Biology, Pennsylvania State University
http://www.bio.psu.edu/People/Faculty/Fisher/cold_seeps/

Colligan, Douglas, "Decompressing with Robert Ballard: An Interview with the Scientist Who Discovered the Titanic," Omni Magazine online
http://www.omnimag.com/titanic/deep/ballard/1.html

"Explorations," the Ocean Explorer Web site maintained by the National Oceanic and Atmospheric Administration that allows readers to follow the ongoing adventures of scientists exploring the deep
http://oceanexplorer.noaa.gov/explorations/explorations.html

"Extreme 2000: Voyage to the Deep," an educational project sponsored by the University of Delaware Graduate College of Marine Studies and Sea Grant Program, WHYY-TV, and the National Science Foundation
http://www.ocean.udel.edu/deepsea/level-2/geology/deepsea.html

"The Grave of the Titanic," Web site sponsored by the Gulf of Maine Aquarium

    http://octopus.gma.org/space1/titanic.html

Kinder, Gary, "The Billion Dollar Boat," originally published in *Outside Magazine* (June 1998)

    http://web.outsidemag.com/magazine/0698/9806boat.html

Kunzig, Robert, "Expedition to the Bottom of the Deep Blue Sea," originally published in *Discover*, volume 22, number 12 (December 2001)

    http://www.discover.com/dec_01/featsea.html

MacKay, Mary and Stan Zisk, "Radar and Sonar: A Primer for the Geophysically-Challenged." Hawaii Center for Volcanology

    http://www.soest.hawaii.edu/GG/HCV/NEWSV2N1/mackay1.html

Meadows, Robin, "Aliens in Our Cells," originally published in *Zoogoer* (May/June 1996)

    http://www.fonz.org/zoogoer/zg1996/zgaliens.htm

Meadows, Robin, "Life Without Light: Discoveries from the Abyss," originally published in *Zoogoer* (May/June 1996)

    http://www.fonz.org/zoogoer/zg1996/zglight.htm

Svitil, Kathy, "Black Smokers," *Savage Earth* Web site sponsored by the PBS television station Thirteen WNET, New York

    http://www.pbs.org/wnet/savageearth/hellscrust/html/sidebar2.html

"Technology: Submersibles: Alvin," the *Ocean Explorer* Web site maintained by the National Oceanic and Atmospheric Administration

    http://oceanexplorer.noaa.gov/technology/subs/alvin/alvin.html

"Why Is the Ocean Blue?" *Neptune*'s Web site sponsored by the Naval Meteorology and Oceanography Command, Public Affairs Office, Stennis Space Center, Mississippi

    http://pao.cnmoc.navy.mil/educate/neptune/quest/seawater/blue.html/sidebar2.html

Selected Bibliography

BOOKS

Ballard, Robert D., with Malcolm McConnell. *Adventures in Ocean Exploration: From the Discovery of the Titanic to the Search for Noah's Flood.* Washington, D.C.: National Geographic, 2001.

Cramer, Deborah. *Great Waters: An Atlantic Passage.* New York: W.W. Norton, 2001.

Duxbury, Alyn C., Alison B. Duxbury, and Keith A. Sverdrup. *An Introduction to the World's Oceans.* 6th edition. New York: McGraw Hill, 2000.

Hoyt, Erich. *Creatures of the Deep: In Search of the Sea's "Monsters" and the World They Live In.* Buffalo, NY: Firefly Books, 2001.

Kinder, Gary. *Ship of Gold in the Deep Blue Sea.* New York: Atlantic Monthly Press, 1998.

Kunzig, Robert. *Mapping the Deep: The Extraordinary Story of Ocean Science.* New York: W.W. Norton, 2000.

Tarbuck, Edward J., and Frederick K. Lutgens. *Earth Science.* 9th edition. Upper Saddle River, NJ: Prentice Hall, 2000.

Thompson, Tommy. *America's Lost Treasure.* New York: Atlantic Monthly Press, 1998.

Weiner, Jonathan. *Planet Earth.* New York: Bantam Books, 1986.

WEB SITES

Conger, Krista, illustrated by Zeke Smith, ''Killer Surf,'' Students in the Science Communications Graduate Studies Program at the University of California, Santa Cruz: Science Notes 1999

http://scicom.ucsc.edu/SciNotes/9901/kill/kill.htm

Embley, Bob, "Sea Floor Mapping," National Oceanic and Atmospheric Administration Ocean Explorer Web site

http://oceanexplorer.noaa.gov/explorations/lewis_01/background/seafloormapping/seafloormapping.html

"Gold Bug Shed's Light on How Some Gold Deposits Formed"

http://www.spacedaily.com/news/early-earth-01j.html

"The Jason Project"

http://www.jasonproject.org/jason_project/jason_project.htm

Kunzig, Robert, "A Thousand Diving Robots," Discover Magazine online originally published in *Discover*, volume 17, number 4 (April 1996)

http://www.discover.com/archive/index.html

Lemonick, Michael D., "The Last Frontier," Time Magazine online archives, originally published in *TIME*, volume 146, number 7 (August 14, 1995)

http://www.time.com/time/magazine/archive/1995/950814/950814.cover.html

"Life as We *Didn't* Know It," Science@NASA, a Web site that helps the public understand how exciting NASA research is

http://science.nasa.gov/headlines/y2001/ast13apr_1.htm?list52260

"Marine Environmental Geology: Fluid Flow from Accretionary Prisms—Aleutian Trench and Cascadia Margin"

http://www.geomar.de/sci_dpmt/umwelt/ropos_kodiak/

"Scientists Discover Secrets of 'Lost City': New class of hydrothermal vents formed differently," National Science Foundation press release, July 11, 2001

http://www.nsf.gov/od/lpa/news/press/01/pr0156.htm

Siegel, Lee J., "Café Methane," NASA Astrobiology Institute News Archive, November 30, 2001

http://www-space.arc.nasa.gov/ezine/articles/seeps.html

"Technology: Submersibles: *Alvin*," National Oceanic and Atmospheric Administration Ocean Explorer Web site that gives the history of *Alvin*, the most famous submersible

http://oceanexplorer.noaa.gov/technology/subs/alvin/alvin.html